Replenish The Earth

The Ministry Life Cycle

"Introduction
to the
Ministry Life Cycle"

By

Dr. Laura Thompson

Copyright, 2009

AMC World, Inc.

First published 2009

Copyright © Dr. Laura Thompson 2009

ISBN # 978-0-9720750-5-3

All rights reserved. Without limiting the rights under copyrights reserved above, no part of this publication may be reproduced, stored in or introduced into a retrieval system, or transmitted, in any form or by any means (electronic, mechanical, photocopying, recording or otherwise), without the prior written permission of the copyright owner.

Formatted using Open Office

Printed and bound in the United States of America

www.amc-world.com

Acknowledgments

I would first like to acknowledge God my creator who took the time to create me, not just once, but time and time again. He didn't just leave me spinning on the wheel. He molded me, and shaped me in a way so unique, that the gift he gave me could only fit in my vessel. If taken out and given to someone else, the gift would come as a sounding brass, a tinkling cymbal or an uncertain sound. My parents, Levi & Desrene Thompson have been at the core of my creative awareness. They never put a damper on the discovery of my intrinsic talents and abilities. Instead they encouraged me to pursue all that was in me. As a result, they were often shocked at the manifestation of things that emerged from this empty vessel. God can do anything.

While there are numerous mentors I'd like to thank (and they know who they are), I instead would like to give thanks to God for all of the trials, troubles and tribulations I encountered on this path. For without them I would not have a testimony. They served to test my character and the witness of the Holy Spirit within me. Today, I am the victor of my circumstances & experiences – not the victim.

I'd also like to extend special thanks to a dear friend who gave me the freedom to separate myself to God in order to produce this work. I really appreciate the sacrifice you've made during a very crucial time in your life and development. God who sees in secret will reward you openly.

I would also like to extend thanks and appreciation for the contributions made by Bishop Gladstone Royal, Mr. Floyd Muir of G & F Records, and Merlyn Ipinson Flemming of Emerge Me.

Replenish the Earth

The Ministry Life Cycle

By Dr. Laura A. Thompson

Table of Contents

Acknowledgments 3
Preface 9
Lesson 1 – Loss & Separation 11
Lesson 2 – From Isolation to Disconnection 21
Lesson 3 – Atmosphere for Birthing 27
Lesson 4 – Obedience 29
Lesson 5 – Coming Together 31
Lesson 6 – Using Language 33
Lesson 7 – The Dark Places 35
Lesson 8 – Alignment 37
Lesson 9 – Obstacles 39
Lesson 10 – Being Balanced 41
Lesson 11 – Identity 47
Lesson 12 – Consecration 49
Lesson 13 - Jesus in the Temple (Material Possessions) 51
Lesson 14 – Prayer – Garden of Gethsemane 53
Lesson 15 – It's a Matter of Time 57
Lesson 16 – It's Time to Heal 61
Lesson 17 – Tragedy 63
Lesson 18 – The Dark Places 65

Preface

If ministry is indeed a life cycle, then it functions based on business and the principles of growth. The concept of cycles assumes that each stage can be perpetual/ongoing. Cycles continue over and over. The idea that life is a cycle denotes that it has a continuing growth factor. It is not possible to have life without creation and growth. After a person place or thing has reached a certain stage in development, a measure is assessed. In fact, measures are assessed throughout the process to determine normal and abnormal growth.

Most of what is written is based on the culmination of experiences and or observations made as people stepped into ministry. It is important to be intimately exposed to ministry behind the scenes. As you read of testimony and experiences both seen and felt, the intention is to introduce varying and sometimes narrow viewpoints, which will become cause in the matter of readers to take an introspective look at ministry within their own lives.

To minister is an act of the heart and comes from love and sacrifice for the betterment of people and for the fulfillment of purpose on the earth. Before one can get to "ministry" a link must be established between purpose and the gift(s). This book focuses a lot on gifts. I've been blessed with several gifts, which I choose to use for the purpose of building the kingdom of God. My heart is toward the souls of men and what can be done to restore those souls back to God – creator and giver of life.

Lesson 1 – Loss & Separation

The year my father died was a year of transition for me. Not only did I have to learn to live without his leadership and guidance, but I also went from receiving nearly 7 streams of income to receiving next to none. In addition, my music mentor plus 9 other significant people also passed away that year. And while the death of my father and the change in my finances were two mutually exclusive events (one having nothing directly to do with the other), I felt as if I'd been on this path before. The feeling of being permanently separated from the familiar became familiar to me.

[Separate ye Paul and Barnabas for the work I have set for them – Acts]

What appeared as a time of continual loss, slowly turned to an opportunity to gain perspective on self and what the creator had destined for me to do. I've dabbled at lots of interesting pursuits in my lifetime. And while I haven't had this level of significant loss in my life before, the experience immediately reminded me of a time, a cycle – 10 years ago, which led to the release of my first music CD.

Song writing and poetry were part of my gifts and abilities since I was 8 years old. I entered and lost my first music competition at the age of nine. Now that I think of it, the accomplishment I made was pretty remarkable for a kid. The accomplishment: I sang and I accompanied myself on piano while reading sheet music and lyrics, which I wrote. My competitor, on the other hand had one of the judges play for her while she sang. The judges' comments mainly dealt with metronome timing, and my lack of eye contact with the audience. Remarkable performance, but it was not enough for a win to the judges. My first heartbreak – the loss was supposed to be enough to stop me from singing permanently. Even now I say to myself, why did God allow this to happen, and further, why didn't I give up? I mean I would love to actually win at something in life – I thought. So I kept trying. For some strange and unknown reason, I never gave up.

Assignment Week 1 – Driving Force

For this assignment you'll be required to write a paragraph describing forces that drive you to keep you going. Think of a time before the age of 12 where you were driven to do something. Briefly describe the event.

What were you driven to do at that age? Define/Describe the force (enabling factor) that caused you to do the thing you were driven to do. How did you feel at the end? What sense of accomplishment did you experience?

Paul the Apostle said

"I press toward the mark for the prize of the high calling of God, in Christ Jesus"

(Philippians 3:14)

If a person is doing the work of pressing, or pursuing, there has to be some form of resistance – whether internally or externally, that is going in the opposite direction of the effort to press or pursue.

Assignment Week 2 – Resistance

Instructions: Find two people in the Bible who had to press against some sort of resistance. Write a news broadcast describing the play of events that occurred in the lives of these people. You can present your findings in the form of a PowerPoint presentation. Choose an audio media option to record your broadcast. Be prepared to orally present your broadcast to the class and to comment on the broadcasts from other students.

Most times, people allow the press to overtake them – disabling them from reaching their goals in a timely fashion. Many die before actualizing their dreams. Consequently the earth's soil is rich with talents that have not been actualized. Work and work environments in certain doses, along with a lack of clear vision has tendency to cause people to miss opportunities to pursue deeper potential. If not careful, a lifetime is lived without regard to the creator's purpose for living, causing the created to feel totally unfulfilled.

This was almost my testimony. Early on in life, I

drenched myself in a work environment that occupied much of my time. The diagnosis was simple. I became annoyed because so many years and so much time had been spent accumulating songs and researching the Bible. It was time to record the material. I had the money but I worked so much that I lacked the time to go into the recording studio. I had to make a choice.

God presented an open door and he closed another. The open door required faith to walk through it. I had to have the faith to walk through the door before it actually closed. Sometimes God closes the door and it's evident that you need to go in another direction. Other times, he asks us to take him at his word and walk through even though the door is not physically closed yet. Missed opportunities cause people to experience the deepest regret. Opportunities when paired with preparation enable people to experience the greatest enrichment of life. However, missed opportunities can present themselves as a resulting of the lack of faith in this area.

Sometimes we stay at the same place too long – failing to seize the day because of fear, doubt, unbelief, low self-esteem or low self-image. There are opportunities to get a fresh start, as well as there are opportunities to run from significantly bad situations. At times we get comfortable with the familiar and lose sight of where God is leading us. The stench of the familiar can be paralyzing to the nostrils, and demobilizing to the zeal required for the hour.

Timing is everything. In Esther 4:14 Esther almost missed the opportunity to rescue herself and her countrymen. If she did not take the time to go before the King, many would have been lost. The area you are in may be comfortable at the time, but "a little folding of the hands" is usually the prelude to poverty and eventually death (Proverbs 6:10).

Assignment Week 3 – True Move of God

The move of God often comes with a move from what is comfortable and familiar, to what is plain ole strange. What are your initial views of this statement? Is this always the case? Aside from the example with Abraham below, what scriptures can you find to substantiate your viewpoints?

In Genesis, Abraham was 75 years old when God spoke to him to be separated from his kindred. Even at his age and experience, Abraham heeded the call and timing of God to the saving of his house and his entire generation (Genesis 12:4).

    Many are in corporate bondage and it is time to come out. With this realization came a word from the Lord to me – leave Lodebar (2 Samuel 9: 4 – 6). Leave the familiar. I gave my job two weeks notice and without a lifeline or back up, I left that company. Within months I was transitioned to another state, working for a company making double my salary. The income I received became a seed that I planted into my personal ministry. I used the seed money to complete the recording on my first CD project and started a record label with the income earned from this job opportunity. It became clear that isolation from friends and family was God's agenda for me during that time of transition.

Assignment Week 4 – Isolation

Write about an experience with loss and isolation. Describe the situation/scenario leading to the loss and or isolation. What opened up as a result of this experience? What doors if any were closed? Where there lessons learned that came as a result of the experience? What scripture references stand out resulting from this experience? Set up your draft on the page(s) below then retype your response in a 4 – 6 page paper, double spaced.

_____
_____
_____
_____
_____
_____
_____
_____
_____
_____
_____
_____

Lesson 2 – From Isolation to Disconnection

It's hard to mention Lodebar without talking about David, King of Israel, and Mephibosheth, the lame and last remaining relative of Saul (2 Samuel 9). Both David and Mephibosheth experienced varying levels of isolation. Their stories are a reminder that you can be isolated even when surrounded by a host of people. Societal role models and the rich usually get the attention of the masses, and may even produce an unmerited audience of supporters, and employees. People usually glean towards what they define as success, even if it is gained as a result of family ties. Wealth and spiritual prosperity come at a price that not many are willing to pay. However, many are willing to enjoy the fruits of someone's labor. Even labor by definition cannot come conceptually without the experience toil and pain.

In David's case, pain was experienced as his enemies sought to kill him. It was also painful to be forgotten by his father, Jesse (1 Samuel 16: 11) and scorned by his older brothers (1 Samuel 17: 28). On the other hand,

Mephibosheth's nanny dropped him as a baby while escaping the city. So as a paraplegic, this child was at the complete mercy of caretakers, who provided menial care for their boss, Mephibosheth. Meanwhile, the caretakers took adequate care of themselves as they lived off of his land and inheritance. They took full advantage of the fruit from someone else's labor. However, David and Mephibosheth didn't let the pain they experienced stop them from having success.

Assignment Weeks 5 & 6 – Sit or Serve

In this assignment (which you'll be given two weeks to complete), you'll need to develop the outline for a debate based on the following statement(s): It is better to (sit/serve). Your job is first to choose a side then get together with a group of students in the class. Develop an outline defining the characteristics of the individual who is sitting or serving (with your side being the more dominant/favorable than the other). Provide scriptural references, sociological and psychological scenarios where applicable. The final deliverable should be a group PowerPoint presentation and a 3 – 5 page group report describing in detail the factors associated with each side. Use the section below to begin developing the outline or for brainstorming critical factors that should be considered.

It is normal for people to gravitate towards people, places, and things that resemble success and positivity. In school we're introduced to success stories in careers and business practices. While it would be quite simple to write about bright futures and the prophecies spoken over my life and the lives of others, this book will focus more on the transitional period between the prophecy and the actualization. The period of time I'm referring to feels like forever, and looks like a picture's negative.

This is the time before the success and the fame. What you do during this time develops character. To some it may be comfortable to not confront the thing that often is confronting them. Others resist being confronted by anything or anyone because they're disconnected to purpose. Something, someone, some story, or some concept became truer than the living reality within. This false sense of reality and some beliefs disconnect individuals from their divine birthright.

Assignment Weeks 7 & 8 – My Negative

During these last two weeks each student will develop their own story of development from a negative to what you are currently or what you hope to become. In this story consider things you've been connected to or disconnected from. Also include the things that were spoken over your life either from birth or at a young age. Where relevant discuss your divine birthright and what it means (if anything) to you. If you have children, identify what you see happening in them. Describe the birthing process both physically and spiritually. Align your writings with the Word of God and use scriptural references and examples to substantiate your views and demonstrate your comprehension of the task assignment. Use the section below to develop your outline (due week 7 of the learning week). Then prepare a 6 – 8 page paper describing your negative. Prepare to orally present your negative during the last week of class.

_____
_____
_____
_____
_____
_____
_____
_____
_____
_____

Lesson 3 – Atmosphere for Birthing

Perhaps you've come to this point in reading and thought, "This has nothing to do with me. I'm far removed (like a distant cousin) from the work of the ministry – I don't even have a ministry. There's nothing wrong with just being saved and going to church, right?" Before we go any further, I'd like for you to do a simple exercise. If you have a cell phone and you are near it, I'd like for you to turn your phone on vibrate. We don't want to respond to every alarm during this exercise.

From the beginning of time until now, God continues to set order. In the midst of darkness and voidness, God moved to reset the atmosphere. God said let there be and there was.

When we allow God to be God – to be on the throne, to be hallowed and worshiped as God, we can set the atmosphere for God to move on our behalf. When the atmosphere is set, through prayer, praise and worship, God moves. He is God our Father, who is in Heaven. Hallowed be your name. Thy kingdom come, thy will be done in earth as it is in heaven.

God uses us as instruments to speak. It is only through his power that we can speak things into existence. We can speak life and we can speak death. For both life and death are in the power of the tongue. But in the dark and dismal areas of your life, let God be God, seated on the throne – high and lifted up. Let his train fill the temple. Let his presence fill the area of your circumstances where there is lack and despondency. Let God arise in your darkest day. REJOICE!
Choose to rejoice!

In the midst of the raging seas in your life, let there be a firmament in the midst of the waters. Don't drown in your troubles. Let God divide the waters. God spoke and it was. God sets order – not your circumstances, not your drought, not your despondency – God sets order, for the earth is the Lord's, the fullness there of, the world and they that dwell there in.

God is the head. We are the body. There is order in this body. These are kingdom principles. From the beginning, God gave Adam dominion over the fowl of the air, the animals and the garden. In that realm whatever Adam spoke – became as he called it. Adam said fish and it was from then 'til now a fish. He said bird and today it is still a bird.

Lesson 4 – Obedience

Failure to obey causes one to lose their position in the kingdom. Adam had to leave the garden. He had two sons outside of the garden. One son committed homicide, killing the other brother, and the surviving son became a vagabond. DISCONNECTED. DISCOMBOBULATED. Cut off from the kingdom – and cut off from the body. Things that are not connected can eventually dry up and fall off.

Perhaps there is something done in the past that you haven't forgiven yourself for. Many have difficulty making the separation between events that occurred and the future we are living in presently. Jacob in the Bible was known for being a trickster, until he made a distinction between the name given to him at birth, and the future he was living in. Mistakes made, are just mistakes. They have no control over you unless control is given to them.

    We have an advocate with the Father in the person of Jesus. What's the sense of having an advocate that will forgive us of our sins if we're just going to hold on to them after they've been forgiven? It is this state of despondency that leaves us disconnected from the father and his love towards us. Like Adam in the garden (after the apple incident) many become in denial of our purpose for living and being.

Lesson 5 – Coming Together

Instead of receiving the call to battle, many choose to remain in the valley of despondency and indifference – <u>full</u> of dry bones – mixed up with similar parts not fulfilling their intended purpose by design.

But there's a word from God for you.
Ezekiel 37

1 The hand of the LORD was upon me, and carried me out in the Spirit of the LORD, and set me down in the midst of the valley which was full of bones,

2 And caused me to pass by them round about: and, behold, there were very many in the open valley; and, lo, they were very dry.

3 And he said unto me, Son of man, can these bones live? And I answered, O Lord GOD, thou knowest.

4 Again he said unto me, Prophesy upon these bones, and say unto them, O ye dry bones, hear the word of the LORD.

5 Thus saith the Lord GOD unto these bones; Behold, I will cause breath to enter into you, and ye shall live:

6 And I will lay sinews upon you, and will bring up flesh upon you, and cover you with skin, and put breath in you, and ye shall live; and ye shall know that I am the LORD.

7 So I prophesied as I was commanded: and as I prophesied, there was a noise, and behold a shaking, and the bones came together, bone to his bone.

8 And when I beheld, lo, the sinews and the flesh came up upon them, and the skin covered them above: but there was no breath in them.

9 Then said he unto me, Prophesy unto the wind, prophesy, son of man, and say to the wind, Thus saith the Lord GOD; Come from the four winds, O breath, and breathe upon these slain, that they may live.

10 So I prophesied as he commanded me, and the breath came into them, and they lived, and stood up upon their feet, an exceeding great army.

11 Then he said unto me, Son of man, these bones are the whole house of Israel: behold, they say, Our bones are dried, and our hope is lost: we are cut off for our parts.

12 Therefore prophesy and say unto them, Thus saith the Lord GOD; Behold, O my people, I will open your graves, and cause you to come up out of your graves, and bring you into the land of Israel.

13 And ye shall know that I am the LORD, when I have opened your graves, O my people, and brought you up out of your graves,

14 And shall put my Spirit in you, and ye shall live,

Lesson 6 – Using Language

Many have been silent long enough. It's time to speak. Speak the word of God into your dry situations. Speak to the situations and relationships that appear to be buried in the grave. God said that he would open the grave and bring you out.

Many have been disconnected for long enough. It's time to come together and cease from being disconnected in the mind and spirit. These bones were separated in the valley but they showed up after the word of God was spoken. They came in preparation for battle.

You've been fragmented long enough. In John 6:12, Jesus said to his disciples, "Gather the fragments that remain that nothing be lost."

Speak to the fragmented pieces of your life. Let the Spirit of God breath into the dry places of your life and live.

Psalm 63:5 – let your soul be satisfied as with marrow and

fatness and your mouth praise Him with joyful lips. Let the marrow and the joints come together in worship to God. Open your mouth and worship God. For it's in Him we live we move and we have our being. To worship you I live. I live to Worship God. How about you?

Lesson 7 – The Dark Places

Who are you and who are you being in the dark places?

I am reminded of Jason Bourne in the movie, *The Bourne Identity* (2002). In search for his true identity, the actor ends up in a place where he's questioned about who he is. He's incoherent and very concerned about his safety. At the start of this movie, Jason is too weak and disoriented to rationalize the question. Over time, he realizes that he has skills on fighting and knows how to use sophisticated weaponry. He also knows how to disarm people who have weapons. To not know your true identity can be a dismal experience.

To be poised with power and might while being disconnected from one's earthly assignment, is a mere loss of objectivity and purpose. What's the sense of having a bow and arrow if they're only going to be used to make a quilt? There are more efficient instruments to use to make a quilt. This is what we call purpose without adequate skill. The reverse scenario is also debatable. What is the sense for a skilled archer to shoot a target 75 feet away with a rubber band and a crumpled piece of paper? This is what we call skill without purpose. Somewhere in the individual's development, the mobility is there but the purpose and the passion have not been developed. Many have suffered as a result of not being fully developed in life and in ministry. The growth process needs to take a full effect in a person to avoid misalignment of purpose and skill. For whatever reason, examples of misalignment are on display weekly and are readily available for discussion and consumption by many.

Lesson 8 – Alignment

Misalignment occurs when the thing on the inside does not match up with what's on the outside. On the outside, an individual may look like they have everything they need for survival, but the truth can be that the person is extremely broke, busted and disgusted. A person could look like they should know and understand the word of God but on the inside they are clueless of the principles of the Bible or its books. Someone could be dressed up as if they are the pastor, but after careful inspection, you discover that they have not experienced the gift of salvation. How does one expect to really minister effectively when there is no connection to who they are?

When a person does not know who they are, they become a chameleon, like their environment. If surrounded by darkness, the individual becomes as if he or she is a member of the dark. Even bread when not surrounded by adequate light over a period of time, takes on the characteristics of an organism that grows in the dark.

There are several definitions of the word Growth. Some

of the definitions I've found from the Info please website include the act or process, or a manner of growing; development; gradual increase; size or stage of development; completed development, also something that has grown or developed by or as if by a natural process. Based on these definitions, one could say that growth is the representation or development from one stage to another –whether good or bad.

From a spiritual standpoint, it's imperative that Christians identify where they are in their individual stage of the growth process. In order to be like Christ, we have to understand the stumbling blocks that inhibit our growth and potential. It becomes increasingly difficult to move from one stage to the next when there are obstacles present.

Lesson 9 – Obstacles

What is the function of an obstacle then? An obstacle attempts to detract us from reaching our goal or our full potential. Goals set a target and identify where we are supposed to be. Our spiritual goal then is to be like Jesus. This idea is emphasized in many symbols and songs. One symbol created by a man named *Lance Armstrong* contains the letters **WWJD**, which stands for "What Would Jesus Do". Many of you have seen this symbol on key chains, on shirts and on car bumper stickers. Perhaps some of you may have missed the boat on that, and prefer to sing the refrain of the song "To be like Jesus, to be like Jesus, all I ask is to be like him. All through life's journey from earth to glory, all I ask is to be like him." And while the societal symbolism is cute and the request in that song is sincere, often we find that we "fall short" from meeting this goal.

People that fall short of the goal become *connoisseurs* of making excuses for not being like Jesus. And you've heard the excuses. They sound like this: "I'm human…I need a break…I'm tired…I have to eat breakfast so I can't fast…I'm thirsty, I've got to drink something or I really don't have the time. These excuses and others like them tend to draw us away in our own lusts. They produce lasciviousness.

They take us away from the united front we should have to combat the forces of the enemy. It is during times of separation that we become plagued with negative thoughts and feelings toward ourselves and toward our brethren. Our priorities have to be balanced.

1 Timothy 6: 8 – 10, states (English Standard version):

[8] But if we have food and clothing, with these we will be content. [9] But those who desire to be rich fall into temptation, into a snare, into many senseless and harmful desires that plunge people into ruin and destruction. [10] For the love of money is a root of all kinds of evils. It is through this craving that some have wandered away from the faith and pierced themselves with many pangs. Having balance is essential in everything we possess and in everything we do.

Lesson 10 – Being Balanced

The first part of Matthew 6 verse 24 states: [24]No one can serve two masters; for either he will hate the one and love the other, or he will stand by and be devoted to the one and despise and be [s] against the other. (Amplified Version) The things we place as priorities and the excuses we make in life can lead us to walk away in our own lusts. Galatians 5:16 (KJV) says, [16] This I say then, Walk in the Spirit, and ye shall not fulfill the lust of the flesh.

[17] For the flesh lusteth against the Spirit, and the Spirit against the flesh: and these are contrary the one to the other: so that ye cannot do the things that ye would.

The imbalance presented in verse 17 is the reason behind the excuses. A social excuse then is one where society and the person's social surroundings back off, leaving the person to his or her issue. The person making the excuse is no longer bothered by friends, family and society, because the excuse is made in attempts to be unsocial or un-acquainted with responsibility. I got them all the time from my former college students. Their course syllabus stated there's a major midterm exam on week 4 of the semester. They knew from the beginning of the semester that there was an exam. When midterm week 4 came, I'd get an excuse –I have military orders to leave the country. Consequently, the students making the social excuse have military order every 8 weeks (when there's something they're responsible for) but never leaves, nor are they enlisted in the military. Or they'd say, I had a car accident, and mind you this accident only occurs habitually when the student has something important to do – like an exam. Who are we kidding when we use these social excuses to forsake the pursuit of God and purpose? If you walk in excuses, then

> All the social excuses and the things you can't do will only amount to the gum that's on the back of a shoe.

Let's analyze the qualities of *gum* on the back of a *shoe*. Now, many can relate to the disdain and displeasure associated with this presentation, because you've been here before. Well, the truth is, as long as one is still (stagnant, not moving, not progressing) there really is no problem with gum on the back of a shoe. Why? Because at this phase, there is no movement or progression. But once a person decides to <u>get up</u> from point A and move toward point B, he or she will soon recognize that there's a problem or an inhibition.

Gum sticks. It restricts consistent movement. Gum leaves residue and it's often difficult to remove. The gum is that issue that sticks to you. Because the issue, I mean gum is stuck to you, it eventually gets stuck on just about everything you connect to, be it the ground, the carpet, clothes, your hands, your hair, other people. This issue (I mean the gum), infects whatever you touch or connect with. If it gets on the carpet, you have to use a product called 'gum out' to get it out. Sometimes it will come out of clothes with several washings and scrubbings. Some people go to sleep with their issue, (I mean gum) in their mouths. As they wake up, they discover that the gum has moved on.

For example, I used to baby sit two little girls, and one of them (Hillary) forgot to take out her chewing gum before she went to sleep. In the middle of the night, Hillary wakes up crying with an issue. Her chewing gum was tangled near the roots of her beautiful, long, blond hair. She wasn't crying for pain. She cried because this happened to her before, and when it happened she had to get her hair cut off.

Naturally, the solution is to either get rid of the issue; (I mean the gum) or get rid of the hair. Mark 9:43 recommends that drastic measures be taken. It states: And if thy hand offends thee, cut it off: it is better for thee to enter into life maimed, than having two hands to go into hell, into the fire that never shall be quenched:

So Hillary figured that I'd cut off her hair. But, I had a better solution –peanut butter. If you apply peanut butter to the sticky mess, the gum slides out with ease. She got to keep her hair after washing it.

The good news I have for you today is that <u>God doesn't just leave us stuck in the stuff he sent his Son to set us free from</u>. The practice of the world is to lead you to a place, and then leave you stuck there. But according to Psalms 23, the Lord I serve is my Shepherd, and I want for nothing. He leads me, he restores, and yea though I walk <u>through</u> the valley, there's nothing to be afraid of because he's with me.

In our stages of growth and spirituality, it's important to identify where we are and what we need. Examine your self and see where you are with your relationship with God. Weigh yourself in the balance and find out where you are lacking –do you need to fast, or pray or get closer to God? What stage are you at, and what do you require to make it through that stage?

With this, there are four stages of growth and development that I'd like to focus on as they relate to the life of Jesus. While on the road to being like Jesus, perhaps we can apply some of his examples to our personal growth and development. Abraham Maslow said it this way.

A musician must make music, an artist must paint, a poet must write, if he is to be ultimately at peace with himself. What a man can be, he must be.

It's time to show your true identity.

Lesson 11 – Identity

For twelve years, Jesus functioned under what many thought was his true identity. He was the son of a carpenter, right? Well, as with everyone, there comes a point in <u>time</u> when you need to set the record straight and come to grips with who you are and whose you are. Else, living in a state of denial often causes an identity crisis. People that go through this experience don't know who they are or why they're here. You know, people that live to please people (people pleasers) want to make sure everyone is happy so they don't rock the boat or be the cause of instability. Now the scripture does not imply that you take all of twelve years to find out who you are in God. In fact, the sooner you hear from God, receive confirmation through the Spirit and in the word about your purpose in life, the better off you'll be and the less you'll depend on hearing a "prophetic word from people".

In <u>Luke 2:49</u>, ***Jesus as a boy in the temple said to his earthly parents,*** How is it that ye sought me? wist ye not that I must be about my Father's business?

The message version says it this way: Why were you looking for me? Didn't you know that I had to be here, dealing with the things of my Father?"

Jesus was not referring to his earthly father, the carpenter. It's one thing for people to say who you are, but there comes a time that you need to speak for yourself. I must be about my father's business.

Lesson 12 – Consecration

As Jesus grew, the Spirit that descended on him as a dove (now within him) recognized he needed to draw away to consecrate himself through fasting –not eating for 40 days. What was the challenge? The challenge was against his identity.
Matthew 4:3 in the Amplified Bible states:
³ And the tempter came and said to Him, If You are God's Son, command these stones to be made [loaves of] bread.
This is why it's important to know and understand the word of God and how his word applies to your calling and your purpose. We as Christians are under the attack of the enemy, who challenges our stand for Christ.

But when you have done all to stand, Ephesians 6 says stand, having your loins gird about with truth, and the breastplate of righteousness and the shield of faith –there with enabling you to stand against the wiles or the tricks of the enemy.

What is a fast and why do we need to fast? When temptations come, we need to already be prepared for them.

Fasting helps us submit our ways and habits to God. Fasting also disciplines us – drawing us closer to God in preparation for future events and situations (both good and bad).

Lesson 13 - Jesus in the Temple (Material Possessions)

Once a person identifies who he/she is in Christ and disciplines self by drawing close to God through fasting, that person can walk in the Spirit and make a clear distinction between the spiritual and the material. There's a clear distinction between what's clean and what's dirty. When this distinction is made, a cleansing of the temple becomes necessary. The sight of ungodliness stirs up that person's righteous indignation. The prophet, Jeremiah first saw this through his spiritual eyes in Jeremiah 7:10 – 12 (Amplified Version) which says:

[10] And [then dare to] come and stand before Me in this house, which is called by My [a] Name, and say, [By the discharge of this religious formality] we are set free!--only to go on with this wickedness and these abominations?

[11] Has this house, which is called by My Name, become a den of robbers in your eyes [a place of retreat for you between acts of violence]? Behold, I Myself have seen it, says the Lord.

[12] But go now to My place which was in Shiloh [in Ephraim],

where I set My Name at the first, and see what I did to it for the wickedness of My people Israel.(A)

This was the reference that Jesus pointed to in Luke 19:45 – 46, which reads (NKJV):

⁴⁵ Then He went into the temple and began to drive out those who bought and sold in it,[a] ⁴⁶ saying to them, "It is written, 'My house is[b] a house of prayer,[c] but you have made it a "den of thieves."'

Lesson 14 – Prayer – Garden of Gethsemane

This leads us to the fourth stage of growth and development as seen in the life of Christ --**prayer**. When all of the heroics, the miracles, and the discussions with people have ended there comes a time in the growth process that we should yearn for something more. There is an eternal connection that should lead us to the throne of our heavenly Father. When the cares of the world get us down and out, we should automatically go to the creator of the world for direction and for inspiration to help us deal with the times and the seasons.

Prayer is essential communication with God. Toward the end of his earthly journey, Jesus was led to the Garden of Gethsemane to pray. We can find the story of Jesus praying in the Garden of Gethsemane in Matthew 26 (NKJV), beginning at verse

^{36} Then Jesus came with them to a place called Gethsemane, and said to the disciples, "Sit here while I go and pray over there." ^{37} And He took with Him Peter and the two sons of

Zebedee, and He began to be sorrowful and deeply distressed. ³⁸ Then He said to them, "My soul is exceedingly sorrowful, even to death. Stay here and watch with Me."

³⁹ He went a little farther and fell on His face, and prayed, saying, "O My Father, if it is possible, let this cup pass from Me; nevertheless, not as I will, but as You will."

⁴⁰ Then He came to the disciples and found them sleeping, and said to Peter, "What! Could you not watch with Me one hour? ⁴¹ Watch and pray, lest you enter into temptation. The Spirit indeed is willing, but the flesh is weak."

⁴² Again, a second time, He went away and prayed, saying, "O My Father, if this cup cannot pass away from Me unless[e] I drink it, Your will be done." ⁴³ And He came and found them asleep again, for their eyes were heavy.

⁴⁴ So He left them, went away again, and prayed the third time, saying the same words. ⁴⁵ Then He came to His disciples and said to them, "Are you still sleeping and resting? Behold, the hour is at hand, and the Son of Man is being betrayed into the hands of sinners.

During a dramatic presentation I saw a few years ago, the final hours of Jesus with his disciples was uniquely depicted. There was heavy emphasis of the sorrow Jesus felt, and while he selected 3 disciples to go further with him in prayer, Jesus found that their flesh took control over them. They were ill-prepared (caught off guard). But Jesus was in tune with the times and the seasons of his life.

The establishment of identity, the consecration through fasting, the ridding of material things and the prayer in the garden of Gethsemane all lead up to Christ's ultimate purpose here on earth – Golgotha. And while there are many more facets of growth that can be examined in the life of Christ, they all lead to a set time, a divine appointment, along the same road, up the same hill – Golgotha.

It's all about the appointed time.

Lesson 15 – It's a Matter of Time

Solomon identified in Ecclesiastes 3:1-4 that

¹To every thing there is a season, and a time to every purpose under the heaven:

²A time to be born, and a time to die;

Jesus was born in Bethlehem in a manger. In moments leading up to his birth, the stars knew when and where to align themselves giving indication to the 'astrologers of the day' that something was about to happen. The wise men stated that they saw the star in the east. There are millions of stars, but the star that showed up in the east knew the exact season when to appear and where to appear.

According to Isaiah 53:2, Jesus grew as a **tender plant**. He grew and developed for approximately 33 years and then it was ***time to die***. There is growth in dying in Christ. Paul states to the Philippians in the 1st chapter, verse 21

–for me to live is Christ and to die is gain.

When Jesus died, the sun *with complete disregard* for its normal course, turned black, and the *veil of the temple* was

torn. Imagine that –the veil of the temple even knew what time it was and stayed in tact until Jesus gave up the ghost.
And then it became what Solomon calls – *a time to plant*.
In John 19:39 – 41 (KJV) it states

> **³⁹ *And there came also Nicodemus, which at the first came to Jesus by night, and brought a mixture of myrrh and aloes, about an hundred pound weight.***
>
> **⁴⁰ *Then took they the body of Jesus, and wound it in linen clothes with the spices, as the manner of the Jews is to bury.***
>
> **⁴¹ *Now in the place where he was crucified there was a garden; and in the garden a new sepulcher, wherein was never man yet laid.***

Now many of us have lost loved ones and have taken them to the grave side watching the burial staff lower the coffins down in the earth. And while the physical body is lowered to the ground, the soul will return to its maker. In fact almost every death before Jesus had the same consequence because death *used to be* **directly** associated with hell. The act of planting is involved – in this case, it's the planting of the body in the ground, returning it to its original form from creation. The funeral staff or minister on hand usually says "Ashes to ashes and dust to dust."

However, in the case of Christ, there was no direct

association between death and hell, because a few decades earlier, one of his earthly grandfathers, David said in Psalm 16:10 "For thou wilt not leave my **soul** in hell; neither wilt thou suffer thine Holy One to see **corruption**." It was time for the earth to give up that which was planted, so up from the grave, Christ arose with power in his hand and the keys. Revelations 1:18 says

> **I am he that liveth, and was dead; and, behold, I am alive for evermore, Amen; and have the keys of hell and of death.**

Thus Solomon declared that it was time to pluck up that which is planted;

³A time to kill, and a time to heal;

Yes, in due time, Jesus was killed but his blood was shed for our healing because according to Isaiah 53:3,

> *he was wounded for our transgressions, he was bruised for our iniquities: the chastisement of our peace was upon him; and with his stripes we are healed.*

Lesson 16 – It's Time to Heal

In John 2:19, Jesus plainly said to the Jews, Destroy this **temple**, and in three **days** I will raise it up. It's all a matter of time. Jesus understood the times. And today, you don't have to weep. You don't have to kill the lamb anymore. You don't have to sprinkle blood over the door. Because someone has taken the place of the lamb and he is the Great I Am.

Today we can laugh and have joy because weeping may endure for a night but Joy comes in the morning. While Solomon did not write the book of Ecclesiastes in direct reference to the life, death, burial and resurrection of Christ, he does admonish that we understand the times, the seasons and the purpose throughout our stages of growth and development. As for Christ our Savior and Lord, if he doesn't do anything else, he's already done more than enough. Jesus identified and fulfilled his purpose on earth so that you can have life and have it more abundantly. What more do you want him to do to prove his love for you? He has done enough.

Lesson 17 – Tragedy

According to Isaiah 6:1, God knows how to provide comfort in difficult times. When going through tough times, we need to enter the presence of God. In the first verse of this chapter, Isaiah sees God. Sometimes it takes tragedy in order to see things more clearly. If we are in a mess, sometimes we won't know it until someone leaves. When we get in the presence of the Lord, things that lie dormant can come back to life, while other things that look alive may actually die as the Lord wills.

During this time in history, Isaiah was the only one recorded in the scripture, who saw the Lord (of all the people that lost their King Uzziah). Seeking the Lord is a personal experience that requires separation (alone time). God is waiting on you to make your appointment with him. The question is, where are you? Ideally, you are in a quiet place seeking the Lord. If you seek Him you will find Him when you search for him with all your heart (Jeremiah 17:17).

In Isaiah 6:5, we see a man looking at his own condition and providing an evaluation of where he is. Isaiah calls himself "undone" and "a man of unclean lips." Adam and Eve saw themselves in the garden as naked when they took their eyes off God. But despite the condition of his heart, Isaiah saw the cleansing power of God. There is a road one must take toward cleansing. When you're acquainted with the cleansing power of God, you can effectively witness with your gift. You can see the world (as Isaiah did in verse 8), see the need, and effectively minister. The condition of the world is dark and should make you uncomfortable. But with compassion, look and remember that God stood with us when we were under development – in our dark places.

Lesson 18 – The Dark Places

To many, the dark place is the place where we sit the longest – under development. It's the point after the picture is captured. It's the place where the picture negative goes through its conversion. Although we live in a day where pictures are developed more quickly through the advent of digital technology, much can be said about the principles of photography. In general, when a picture was taken using an old fashioned camera, a negative was developed. A picture is said to be worth a thousand words.

That being the case, one could imply the potential of a negative is worth at least double the amount of words than a picture. If a negative remains in that form, it is only deemed as a potential picture. It must be handled with extreme caution. In the olden days, the picture developed in a place called the dark room. In the past, negatives were taken there and gradually exposed to the light. The developer would begin to see a representation of the picture's image. This initial presentation, however, is not to be confused with the full picture's potential. Most times, the color appears distorted – not a complete representation of what was originally captured by the photographer. Even children born premature, left in incubation too long will come out deformed. A bird that is engaged for all of its life may never know its real flying potential because its wings are too weak.

www.ingramcontent.com/pod-product-compliance
Lightning Source LLC
Chambersburg PA
CBHW022110160426
43198CB00008B/420